I am Sonam.

I live in Ladakh.

Sonam with her friend, Manish
Lakhani, and her pet dog.

I study in class five.

I also look after my family's pashmina herds.

I am from the Changpa tribe.

We are wandering shepherds.

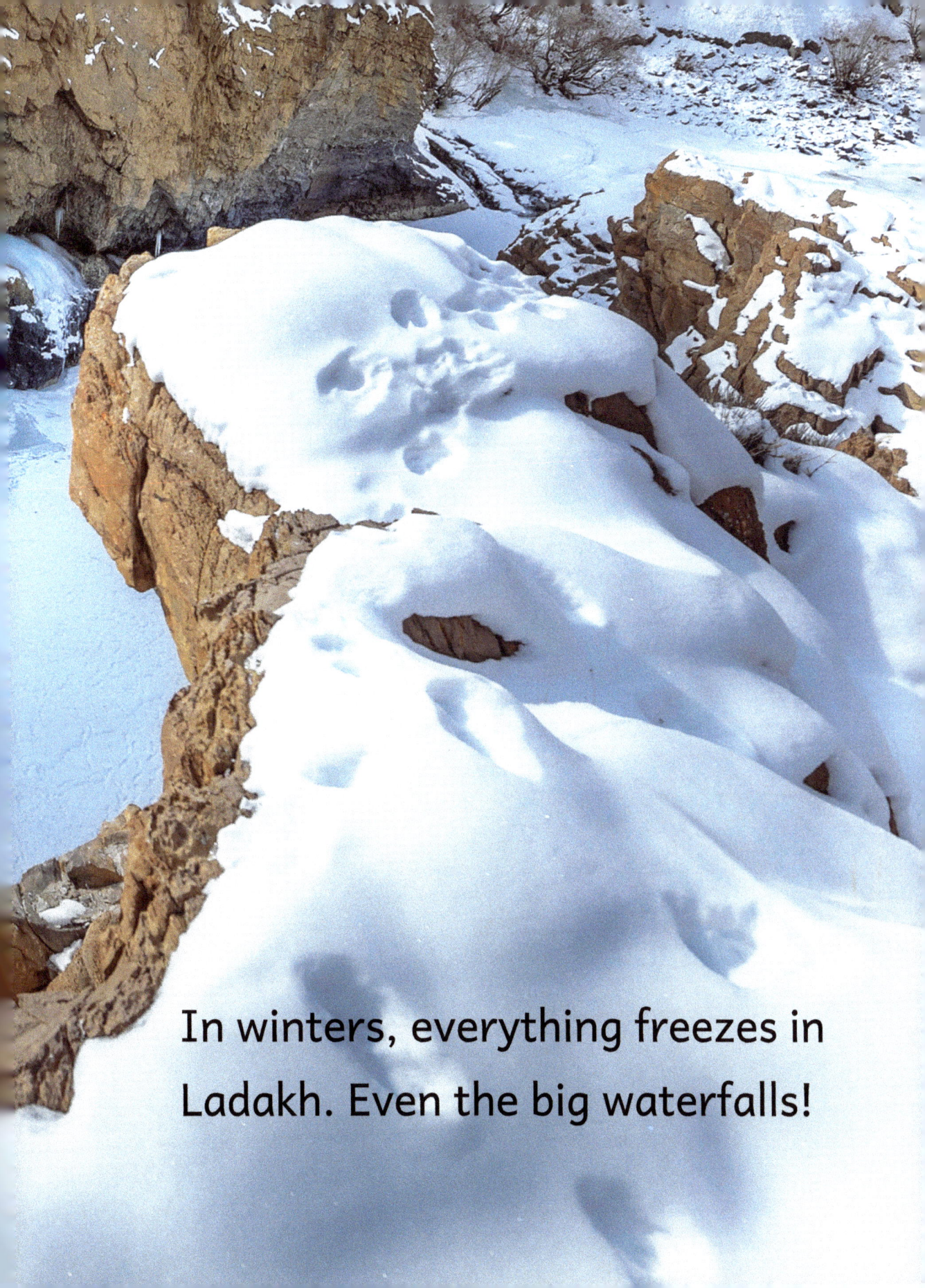

In winters, everything freezes in Ladakh. Even the big waterfalls!

But the summer months are warm and colourful in Ladakh!

This is my favourite lake in Ladakh. The Tso Kar Lake.

I like to play! And my
bicycle is my best friend.

But my little friend, Pema,
loves to play with her pet goat.

My grandmother always says
that sheep and goats and dogs
are better than boxes of money!

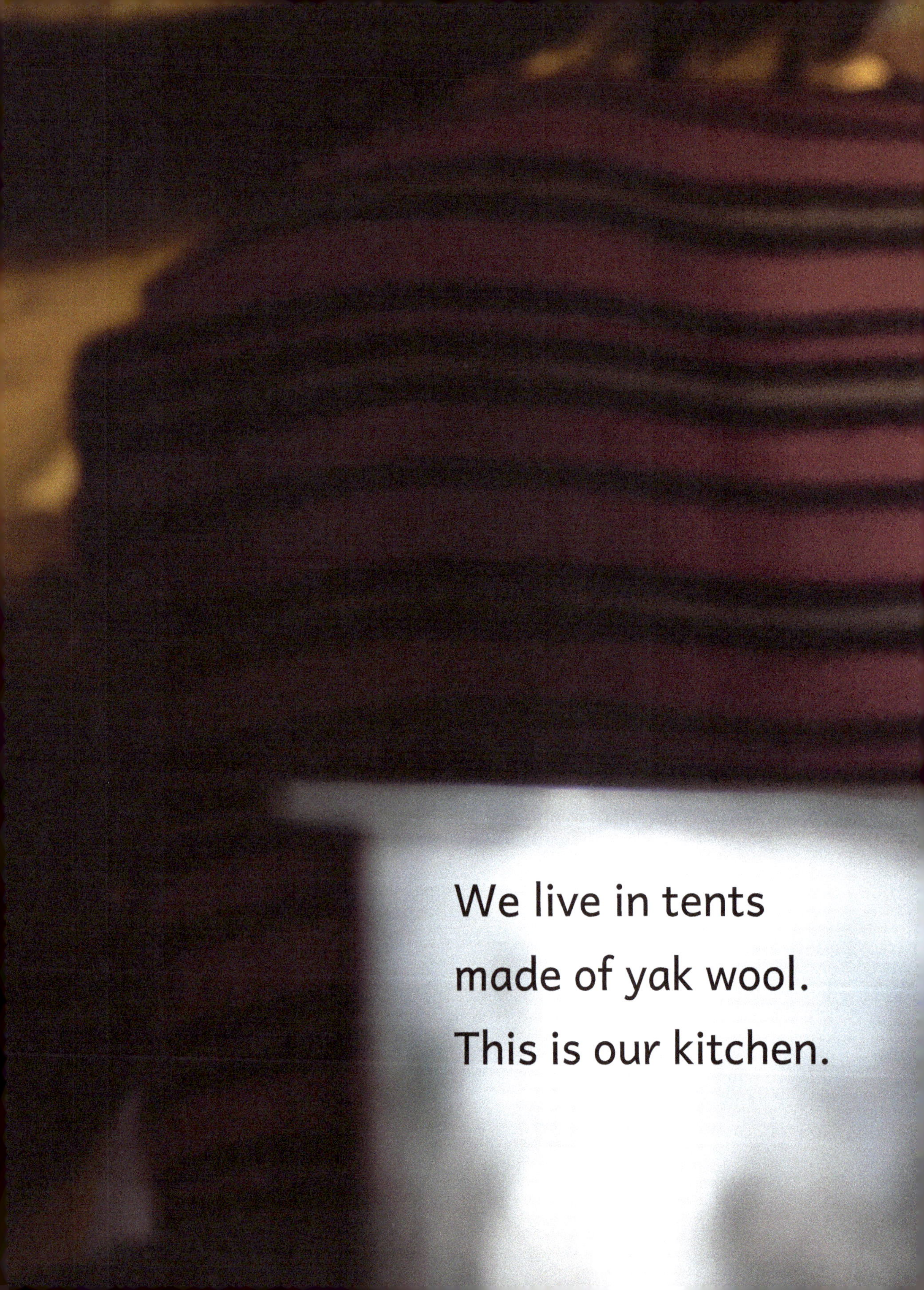

We live in tents
made of yak wool.
This is our kitchen.

Yaks are our friends.

They help us grow food.

There are other
animals in Ladakh too.

The gentle horses.

The rare
Eurasian otter.

And Shanku, the
Himalayan wolf.

There are many monasteries in Ladakh. This is Thiksey Monastery. It is in the Indus Valley.

But the best of all – we have quiet nights in Ladakh, full of stars!

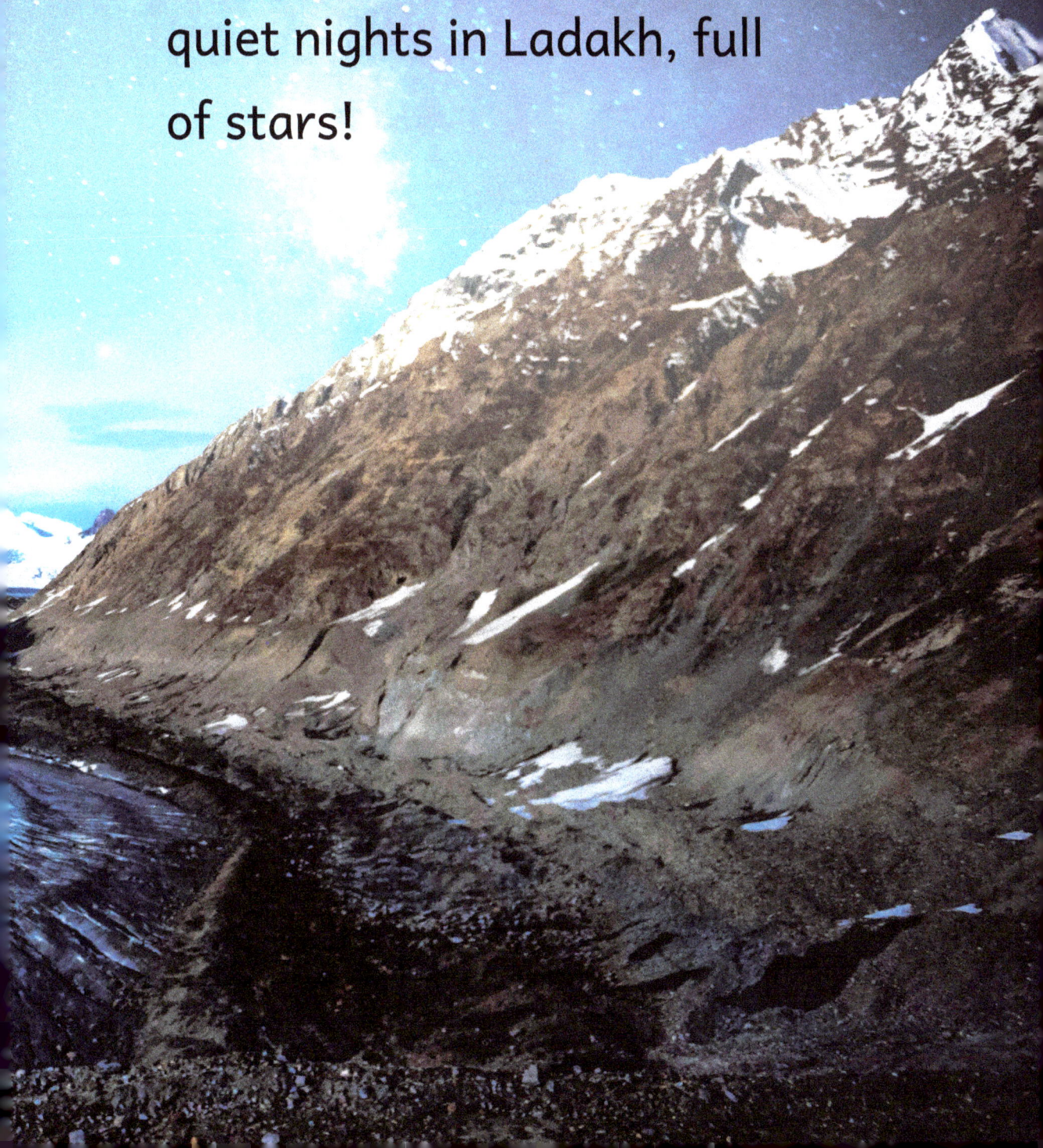

The Heart of the Himalayas!

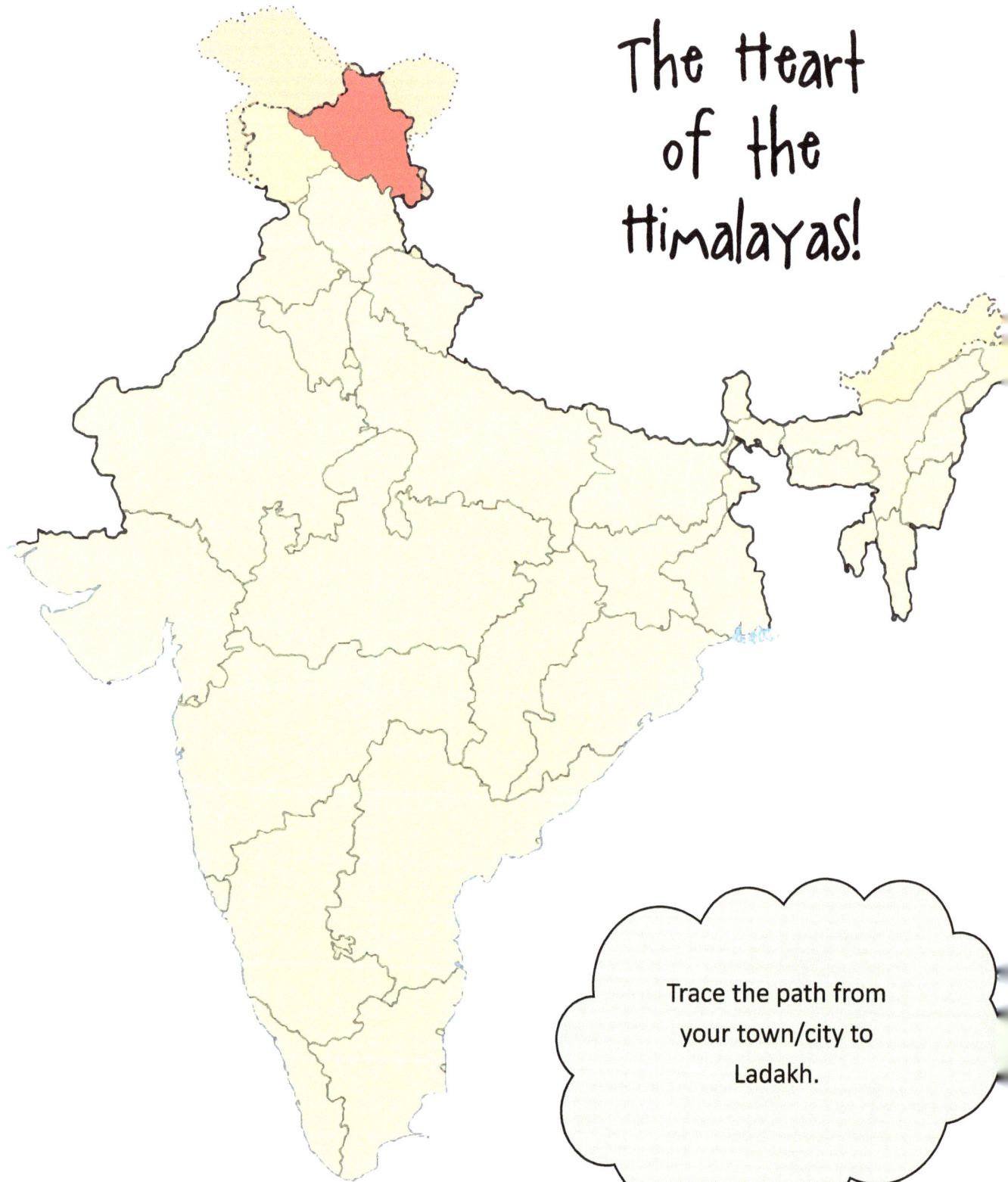

Trace the path from your town/city to Ladakh.

The Changpas

The Changpas are a semi-nomadic tribe. They live in one of the world's coldest deserts—a vast Tibetan plateau in the Himalayas called Changthang that extends from Tibet to Ladakh.

The Changpas roam from one grassy patch to another, trading meat and wool.

The Changpas weave a lot of wonderful things with pashmina and yak wool.

The Changpas grow barley, wheat and peas.

The Melting Glaciers of Ladakh

Ladakh has many glaciers. They are important for all of us. But because of increase in pollution and cutting down of trees, Earth is becoming warmer and the glaciers in Ladakh are melting.

THINK

How can we reduce pollution to stop the melting of glaciers in Ladakh?

ASK

What can we do to take care of our environment?

DISCUSS

With your friends, make a
six-month plan to reduce
pollution.

ACT

Do your bit. Begin with just a few things.

Walk as much as possible, or cycle.

Use less electricity.

Recycle waste.

Use cloth bags. Say no to plastic.

Plant trees.

Buy and eat locally produced food.

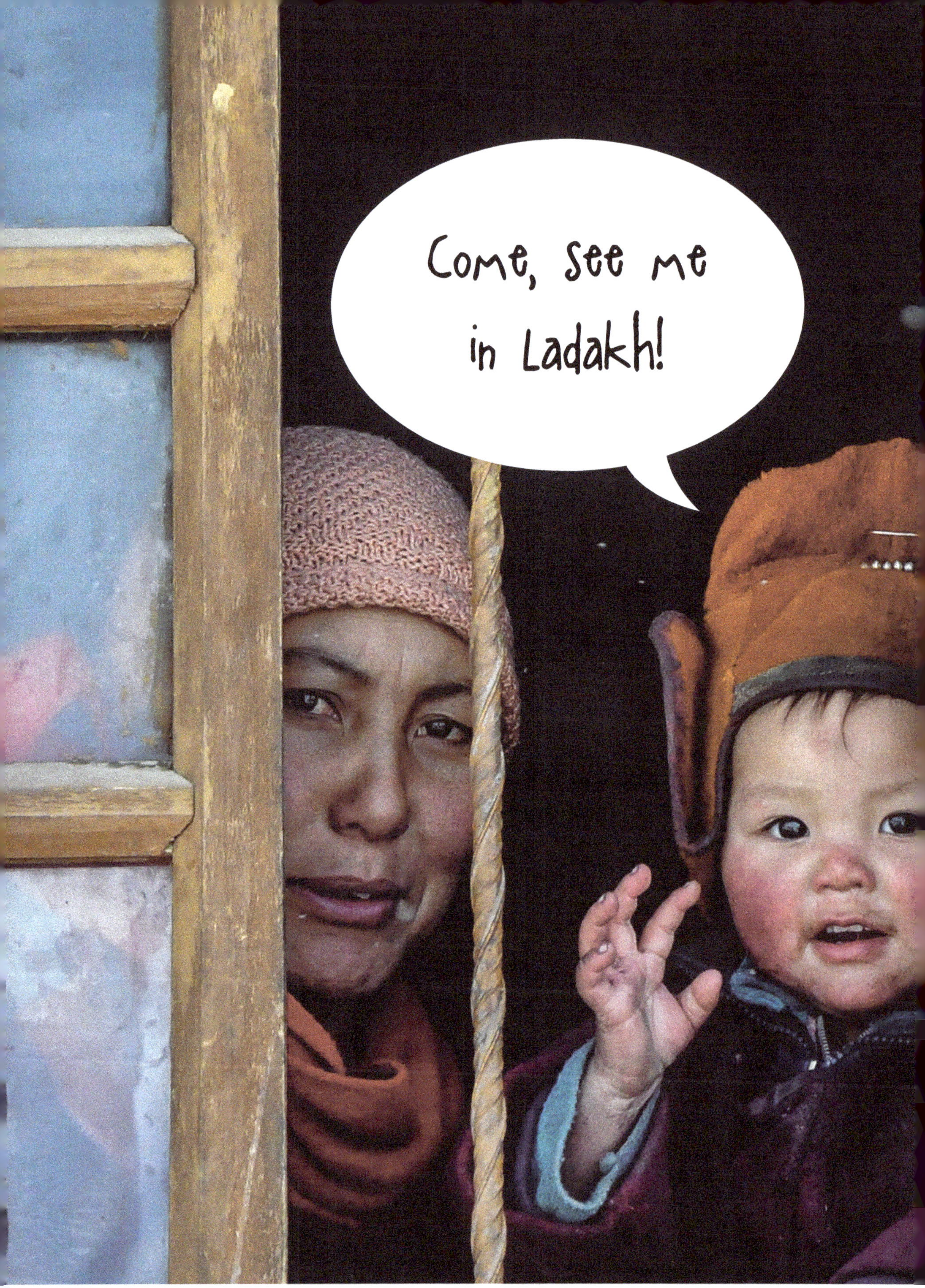
Come, see me in Ladakh!

Manish Lakhani: Photographer and adventure chaser, Manish Lakhani loves his camera, bicycle and the mountains. His love for the mountains has carried him back to Ladakh many times over.

ꖋ KATHA

Katha is a globally recognised non-profit organization (www.katha.org) that has been working in the literacy to literature continuum since 1988. Our nearly 30 years of experience is in publishing and education for children in poverty.

"An educational jewel in India's crown."　　　　**— Naoyuki Shinohara, Deputy Managing Director, IMF**

"Katha stands as an exemplar for all the creative projects around the world that grapple with ordinary and dramatic misery in cities."　　　　**— Charles Landry,** *The Art of City Making*

"Katha has a real soft corner for kids. Which is why it ... create[s] such gorgeous picture books for children."　　　　**— Time Out**

"Katha's work is driven by the idea that children can bring change to their communities that is sustainable and real, just as the children do in [their books.]"　　　　**— Papertigers**

First published by Katha, 2017
Copyright © Katha, 2017
Text copyright © Katha, 2017
Photographs copyright © Manish Lakhani, 2017
A3, Sarvodaya Enclave, Sri Aurobindo Marg, New Delhi 110 017
Phone: 91-11 4141 6600 . 4141 6610 . Fax: 91-11 2651 4373
E-mail: editors@katha.org, Website: www.katha.org

Our Mission: Every child reading well and for fun!
I Love Reading Library is a unique series of books that brings new/ diffident readers into sustainable learning. With high-quality content and design to match the learning needs of children at different reading levels, it brings the best of India's 2000 years of literary heritage. Based on StoryPedagogy devised by Geeta Dharmarajan, these books help increase young readers' ability to understand BIG ideas for change and help them build a kinder, more sustainable world.

ISBN 978-93-82454-53-7

All rights reserved. No part of this book may be reproduced or utilized in any form without the prior written permission of the publisher.

Ten per cent of sales proceeds from this book will support the quality education of children studying in Katha Schools.
Katha regularly plants trees to replace the wood used in the making of its books.

www.ingramcontent.com/pod-product-compliance
Lightning Source LLC
Chambersburg PA
CBHW041634040426
42447CB00020B/3491